# A Brief History
# of Americanism

Other Titles in this Series:

To order these and other AHA publications, visit:

# www.historians.org/AHAStore

# A Brief History of Americanism

by **Kenneth Weisbrode**

Published by the
American Historical Association
400 A Street, SE
Washington, DC 20003
www.historians.org

ABOUT THE AUTHOR: Kenneth Weisbrode is Assistant Professor of History at Bilkent University.

AHA EDITORS: Allen Mikaelian, Liz Townsend

LAYOUT: Chris Hale

ACKNOWLEDGEMENTS: The author is grateful for the thoughtful assistance of the series editors, Sebastian Conrad and Prasenjit Duara, to Chris Hale and Allen Mikaelian, and to the members of the Oslo Contemporary International History Workshop, especially Marc Frey, Vincent Lagendijk, Ingrid Lundestad, Susan Pedersen, Klaus Petersen, Katharina Rietzler, Sissel Rosland, and Hanne Hagtvedt Vik.

ABOUT THE COVERS: The image on the front cover is a birdseye view of the Pan-American exposition, Buffalo, May 1–November 1, 1901; courtesy the Library of Congress Prints and Photographs Division, www.loc.gov/pictures/item/2003674793.

The image on the back cover is a painting of the OAS building in Washington, DC, titled *Heroes and Artists Come to the Pan American Union To Be Consecrated* (1962) by Nicaraguan artist Asilia Guillén (1887–1964). The original painting is part of the collection of the OAS Art Museum of the Americas (gift of José Gómez-Sicre). Image copy is courtesy OAS Museum of the Americas.

© 2013 by the American Historical Association

ISBN: 978-0-87229-207-9

LIBRARY OF CONGRESS CATALOGING-IN-PUBLICATION DATA:

    Weisbrode, Kenneth.

    A brief history of Americanism / by Kenneth Weisbrode.

    pages cm

    Includes bibliographical references and index.

    ISBN 978-0-87229-207-9 (alk. paper)

    1. America—Name. 2. America—History—Philosophy. 3. America—Historical geography. 4. America—In literature 5. Geographical perception—America. I. Title.

    E18.75.W45 2013      304.2'3—dc23      2013027823

# Table of Contents

# The History of Regions in the Modern World

## Series Introduction

Regionalism is a very poorly defined and understood term in the historical literature. In part, this reflects the strong presence of methodological nationalism that dominated historical writing since the 19th century in which the nation was often the unspoken frame of reference for whichever topic was being explored. Ironically, the recent wave of globalization that has been sweeping the world since the end of the Cold War in the last decade of the 20th century, has been accompanied by an almost simultaneous process of region-formation. While this has been most obvious in the case of Europe, it has also appeared in many other parts of the world, including NAFTA in North America, Mercosur in Latin America, and in maritime Asia (ASEAN, East Asia Summit), among others. The new attention to the development of these regions has alerted many to explore the topic historically. What are the historical bases of these regions? Was there a region-making process happening under the radar during the period of high nationalism? What was the relationship of pre-modern empires to networks and connections in regions beyond their administrations? How were regions developed by modern colonial empires which were often dominated capitalist interests who sought to integrate far flung markets? What is the relationship between globalization, regionalism and the nation-state?

By exploring these questions, the series seeks to supply some materials and concepts to grasp this neglected phenomenon suspended between national and local space and the space of globalization and world history in the modern and early modern periods in different parts of the world. The studies here investigate several key dimensions. First they distinguish regions spatially between sub-national and supra-national (or supra-state) regions. This series deals with supra-national regions, although the phenomenon of sub-national areas shaping wider regional networks is an important one. Another important distinction refers to region-making from the bottom-up (often called regionalism) and top-down self-conscious, often ideological and political constructions of regions (sometimes called regionalization). Networks have been found to be among the most important connectors of regions, but these are not necessarily only bottom-up forces. Particularly in the modern period, the latter are subject to political and institutional requirements of territorial states which also shape them. How they negotiate these trans-border regimes is an important historical topic. While bottom-up and top-down approaches focus primarily on forces internal to the region, a third perspective foregrounds broad external processes that not only constrained and limited, but also enabled and spawned region-formation. Regions, while constituting the strategic frame of reference of historical actors, also need to be understood as entities that emerged under the pressures of the international state-system and capitalist integration. In this reading, regionalisms are not only based on shared characteristics, and are not made entirely from within, but are also responses to forces from without and to larger processes of global integration.

Related to these topics is another set of analytical questions: what is the role of economic forces in relation to social, cultural and religious networks? When do political and military contests erupt to control a region? This question rose sharply and devastatingly in World War II when the Germans sought to create a European region under their control and the Japanese sought to do so in East Asia. Finally, there is the matter of cultural regions and their relationship to political and economic factors in creating an identity in a region. Can regions remain spaces of imagination for diverse and heterogeneous groups in a way that the nation is not?

Lastly, we know that historically geography has been a necessary but not sufficient condition for a region. One of the aims of this series is to tackle this tension between physical constraints and the constructed character of the region. Among the factors that have facilitated trans-regional connections and networks, producing regional imaginaries and practices that define the extension of the region, is technology. In the networked and super-speed world of contemporary society is the physical region relevant at all? We believe that physical forms which cross national boundaries — rivers, forests, ecologies, ocean currents—not only remain important, but have become more so as humans have accelerated their degradation and depletion. The regions that have been shaped by this geography– beyond nations—will have to respond to this threat collectively or regionally.

*—Sebastian Conrad and Prasenjit Duara*
*Series Editors*

# I

Tours of Washington D.C. tend to bypass a white, gently ornate building at the corner of 17th Street and Constitution Avenue, Northwest. As tourists migrate from the White House around the Old Executive Office Building toward the National Mall and make the inevitable stop at the Vietnam War Memorial, they often miss this building, set some distance from the street amid gardens dotted with statuary.

It is the headquarters of the Organization of American States, built in 1910 and called the Pan-American Union building and the House of the Americas. Its style is a cross between a Hispanicized Italianate and the standard Washington neoclassical. Made from Andean granite and Georgian marble, it "incorporates design motifs from Aztec, Maya, Toltec and Inca civilizations" as well as reliefs of scenes from the lives of Washington, Bolívar and San Martín, whose overall "effect," according to the diarist, E. J. Applewhite, "is one of invitation; the result is formal but not formidable."[1]

The OAS has 35 members and a broad structure, including a secretariat, an assembly and several councils, committees, specialized conferences and organizations that oversee forums, "dialogues" and technical exchanges with the aim, according to its charter, "to achieve an order of peace and justice, to promote their [member states'] solidarity, to strengthen their collabora-tion, and to defend their sovereignty, their territorial integrity, and their independence." Although not the region's most dynamic organization—Applewhite suggested that an assignment to the OAS is "like watching a painted ship upon a painted ocean"—it is well known in the Western Hemisphere.

The OAS building is symbolic of the city's betwixt-and-between quality, and the idea that the American capital—designed by a Frenchman in the shape of a diamond, set tangentially astride the intersection of the Potomac and Anacostia rivers—is the physical manifestation of a cultural and political compromise. So too is a building that looks both north and south, and represents, in principle at least, a common American home and an Areopagus. It is fitting that the OAS building lies very close to the geographic center of the original federal district. But it is the federal district of the United States of America, not of the Americas.

The historian Alan Henrikson has described Washington D.C. as a cross between an imperial capital and a medium-sized village.[2] "Neither Rome nor home," as locals like to say. Washington is the American capital only in informal parlance; the United States of America is not synonymous with "America," however much the terms America and Americans have come to refer to that country and its citizens.

The meaning of "America" has shifted over time. When, early in the 16th century, the name of the Florentine sailor Amerigo Vespucci was taken by Martin Waldseemüller, a German cartographer, "America" was assigned a place on a map. Later it came to describe the inhabitants of this place, also called "Indians." Only at the turn of the 18th century does one find evidence, first in America itself, subsequently in Europe, of "Americans" referring to people of European descent. Elsewhere in the hemisphere, citizens of the United States are generally called *norteamericanos*, or North Americans—to the displeasure of Canadians, as well as Mexicans, for that matter, who tend to use less flattering but more precise terms: *yanqui* and *gringo*.

The migration of the former term is interesting. Some accounts have it originating in New Amsterdam, later New York, as a Dutch derived appellation: "John Cheese." The cultural and political rivalry between New Englanders and New Yorkers—Yankees and Yorkers—was strong well into the 19th century, and well after the former term had come to describe all Northerners in the language of their Southern enemies. The point which the term traveled beyond North America and acquired a new spelling and meaning for all inhabitants of the United States, including not only New Englanders but also all Northerners and Southerners (as well as "Westerners") is difficult to pinpoint. One suspects that it happened during the final years of the 19th century, in the Spanish-American war. This war brought unity, on the one hand, to the persistent sectional divide in the United States—Northerners and Southerners fought again on the same side and for a single cause, and these children and grandchildren of Civil War veterans had much to prove—and worsened divisions, on the other hand, between the United States and its "Latin" neighbors, whose feelings were mixed over the United States' self-appointed role as defender of all who sought freedom against the tyranny of the Spanish empire in its final throes.

It was also about this time that the United States rediscovered the Western Hemisphere geopolitically and geoculturally, promoting a movement called "Pan-Americanism," which sought to strengthen existing hemispheric ties and to cultivate new ones. Pan-Americanism, however, was neither new nor exclusive among American regionalisms. Similar ideas had existed since the first Europeans traveled across the Atlantic and gave the "New World" historic and, for some, metaphysical, definition. In the writings of Alexander von Humboldt, Carl Ritter and other early geographic thinkers, the Americas acquired a rich character as a zone with inherent, natural features.

To what extent America was "discovered" or "invented" will continue to be a topic for academic discussion, however much the latter verdict appears to have reached a point of consensus.[3] Too often, however, one overlooks that the New World mythology had as much impact upon Europe as it did upon Europe's colonizing efforts in the Americas. "It is for this reason," the historian J. H. Elliott has written, "that America and Europe should not be subjected to a historiographical divorce, however shadowy their partnership may often appear before the later seventeenth century. Properly, their histories should constitute a continuous interplay of two distinctive themes."[4] And alongside the two themes lies an additional paradox: America as the New World redeemer of the Old may have required separation, albeit mythical, but America as the source of infinite riches—a good poor man's country, as William Penn later described it—required numerous intimate connections with Europe and other overseas markets.

Along with God and gold, the adage says, came glory. Over the course of the next two and a half centuries, America and Americanism would be redefined over and again by several generations of thinkers, ideologues, political opportunists and writers. What follows is a brief, synthetic discussion of their ideas and the consequences of those ideas. It aims neither to praise nor debunk, although it does a bit of both through the eyes of its promoters and detractors, but principally to trace some concepts of Americanism in both historic and global context as one of several regionalisms that have played various roles in the modern era.

Why do regionalisms matter? What do they reveal about nation-states and nationalism, empires and imperialism, and about other geographical concepts and ideologies: universalism, "localism" and so forth? To an extent all such identities are invented in a given context in what political scientists call "regime formation." How then may one account for their appeal? How and when do they become self-perpetuating? How and when, in other words, do they come to acquire, advertise and advance "primordial" characteristics? Martin Lewis and Kären Wigen began their celebrated work, *The Myth of the Continents* with the bold statement, "Whether we parcel the earth into half a dozen continents, or whether we make even simpler distinctions between East and West, North and South, or First, Second and

Third Worlds, the result is the same: like areas are inevitably divided from like, while disparate places are jumbled together."[5] But who determines the qualities of affinity, of "like" and "disparate"? Who is to say that certain "peoples . . . stand in special relationship to one another which sets them apart from the rest of the world," or share "a common personality"?[6] How do they adapt, acclimate or otherwise address themselves to rivals? What turns them into one another's foil?

Posing such questions leads to additional, more precise ones about the subject at hand: what exactly is America? Is it consistent with some kind of hemispheric identity, and does that supersede, counteract, or merely exist in parallel with other collective identities? Is it defined more by its distinctiveness from other regions, namely Europe, by its intrinsic consistency, or by a persistent tension between "congruity" and separation?[7] Indeed, does Americanism actually have less to do with the inherent qualities of the Americas than with its status as a transplanted European concept, mystique or ideology? Is it any of these things, or rather something more akin to a tendency, persuasion, disposition, language or discourse? Or, by contrast, is it more powerful, better described perhaps as a philosophy, even a theology? How do these expressions of Americanism compare to other regionalisms, not only to other "pan" movements, but also to broader movements such as Eurasianism, *la francophonie*, et al?

One may attempt to answer these and related questions by dissecting, classifying, analyzing and reconstructing the linguistic and other components of a given regionalism; in that respect Americanism is like any other ideological movement corresponding to territory. It both consolidates and decentralizes large geographic units.[8] But it requires more than ideas in order to do so. It also needs political institutions, trade and population flows, musical and other artistic and literary expressions, along with intangible qualities like friendship and goodwill.[9]

Americanism is regarded by most people to be less "successful" than Europeanism, for example, and probably a good deal more successful than Asianism. In the Orwellian fantasy of a globe divided by macro-regions (where it was part of "Oceania"), America probably comes out, tentatively, somewhere in the middle. But how conclusive are such measurements?

The problem is not simply that comparisons are difficult to make given the almost infinite number of particularities from region to region, but also that the borders themselves are mutable. Lewis and Wigen have proposed regionalism as "a way out" of the metageographical trap, but this requires effort, not least because regional borders are subject to the human imagination, despite their real-world effects. European integration, for example, is regarded by some people, particularly Europeans, to have made a political success during the second half of the 20th century, but not necessarily if one considers Russia, Turkey and several smaller nations excluded from the European Union to be part of Europe, as many Americans and others do. And no matter how much or how little one regards regionalism in Asia as a viable prospect—if one does at all given the many national tensions in that region—few Asians consider the United States to be a true Asian power, and most prefer the term "Pacific" as in "Asia-Pacific," in a similar way that some Americans and Europeans use "Euro-Atlantic." In practice, the preference for more precise territorial definitions signifies a political imperative: to refer to the Euro-Atlantic and the Asia-Pacific suggests a desire for American, specifically US, power to be present in both regions, and to avoid excluding it for want of better terminology. Strictly speaking, the United States is both an Asian and a European power as a result of being a global one. In this respect, no regional idea can prevail entirely on its own terms.

Contending regionalisms in the Western Hemisphere differ significantly over relative success or failure. The judgment is connected to desirability. To the pan-Americanists of the 1890s, a US-led regional bloc was a good thing: not only did it speak to the progressive glory of the American experiment, but also it suited the strategic imperatives laid down by Alfred Thayer Mahan, the Naval War College instructor and leading proponent of *Machtpolitik* in the United States at the turn of the last century. Mahanian strategy looked to the oceans and emphasized the importance of navies and overseas markets. If America (meaning not just the United States, as the term shall be used henceforth) benefited throughout the 19th century from the "free security" supplied by Britain's navy, whose own imperial security in turn depended upon the strength of said navy as well as the so-called balance of power on the European continent, the 20th century demanded a somewhat different calculus. American security continued to prefer "isolation" (understood as insulation) from Europe, namely European conflicts, but also now required a balance of power in Asia, even if this meant the United States had to provide the balance, as well as US hegemony in the Western Hemisphere. "Isolationism" in the United States, in other words, never really applied systematically beyond Europe; in fact several one-time isolationists became ardent "Asia-firsters" once the Cold War set in. Needless to say, such habits and inclinations of power projection did not necessarily sit well with the United States' other neighbors in equal measure. Nobody loves being the object of another, larger power's hegemony, however well mannered. Where one sits in a region determines much of where one stands on the promise and rewards of regionalism. But location is not the only factor.

Regionalism, including Americanism, amounts to much more than a political and psychological report card. It is about more than power. It is also about influence and interchange. And sentiment. It *is* as much, or even more, perhaps, as it *does*. For all that the contemporary world suggests that territory—or more accurately, territoriality, that is to say, the innate and constructed sense of place, of belonging, of identity and so forth—no longer counts for as much as it did before technology shrunk the globe, there still is no uniform global consciousness. Territoriality persists, so much, in fact, that a classic work like Leopoldo Zea's *América como conciencia* (1953) still holds appeal. Its sentiments accumulate as on a palimpsest more than it rises and falls on an historical timeline.

With globalization has come the proliferation of so many networks, however, that a contemporary palimpsest becomes almost impossible to peel back. Fortunately, regionalism benefits from a countervailing tendency, as the sociologists Viviana Zelizer and Randall Collins have noted, to form circuits from networks.[10] Circuits, especially closed circuits, connect familiars; they break down if any one of them leaves the circuit or fails to transmit, unlike the ordinary network, which expands continually through space. A similar process appears to have taken place among nations and regions. When the United Nations was designed at the end of World War II, a great deal of thought went into striking the proper balance between its regional and global (then called "universal") vocations. The latter is generally thought to have won out over the former, with the addition of the powerful Security Council to reassure skeptics that the institution would not go the way of its predecessor, the League of Nations. And so an alliance of the world's most powerful states (as they were in 1945) was fused to a multilateral assembly and a cosmopolitan executive. The proposal to group nations in particular regions to comprise the Security Council or its equivalent—a position advanced by the American diplomat Sumner Welles, whose formative professional experience had been in Latin America—was not pursued.[11] Yet, regional organizations are treated in the UN Charter (Articles 52–54), and the OAS and other groups like the North Atlantic Treaty Organization—modeled initially along the lines of the 1947 Rio Pact—derive their legitimacy from it.

Regional security organizations, as embodiments of what Woodrow Wilson called a security community, are the heirs of empires and of the armed balance of power that Wilsonianism once sought to overthrow. The latter still exists but mainly as a buttress rather than a rival to security communities; so regionalism, at least by the second half of the 20th century and notably in the Euro-Atlantic area, is less an alternative model of world order than a modified synthesis of several pre-existing models.

All this is a way of saying that territoriality still matters a great deal to many people. Yet the village, the town, the city, the province and even the nation-state have become less singular points of identification, while the vast, formerly external realm is still too big for the average consciousness to swallow whole. The majority of the world's citizens are not cosmopolites. A global security community remains, for the time being, a utopia. But regional communities may not be: regional proximity feels natural; regionalism tends to inspire more loyalty than do alliances, blocs, confederacies, systems and other, less integrated, forms of international organization. The historian John Keiger has reminded us, quoting the German geographer Friedrich Ratzel, "that a state's history is always 'a part of the history of neighboring states.'"[12] Most wars happen between neighbors, or when a large state seeks a monopoly on power in a particular region. Close neighbors have the greatest incentives to cooperate. The 3rd-century Indian strategist Kautilya may have been stating a universal truth when he produced the famous dictum, the enemy of my enemy is my friend, but throughout the 20th century, many states have come to realize that his recipe is ill suited to immediate and even more distant neighbors. There is no inherent reason why they all cannot be friends, or at least live at peace with one another.

This was the main lesson of the interwar period: that no single world order is guaranteed to erase enmity between neighbors; peace had to come from the bottom up, as it were, piece by territorial piece. Where this has succeeded in Western and some parts of Eastern Europe, and in a few parts of Asia, it has followed a precedent from the Americas, where "collective security" and a regional community were forged in fits and starts since the early 19th century, albeit under the not always benign umbrella of US power. And while today's OAS is hardly the institution that the EU or even the UN has become, the Western Hemisphere remains one of the world's most peaceful so far as inter-state relations go.[13] This is putting matters in a positive light. Yet, according to many Americans, Americanism is as much about the projection of US power as it is about regional cooperation, let alone solidarity. And this, in turn, is as much a fact as a bias. The United States simply is that much bigger, and so the historical and to some extent the theoretical question is less about what the content of Americanism is than it is whether Americanism has any real and meaningful regional history given the fact that the United States has such disproportionate power relative to other American nations.

There is of course no single region of the world where power is perfectly and equitably distributed. There are almost always sharks amid the minnows. Understanding how they relate to one another does not necessarily imply an endorsement of the imbalance; nor does a reconstruction of the efforts, successful or otherwise, to promote commonalities among them necessarily suggest a *prima facie* repudiation, denial or diminution of underlying political asymmetries. Indeed, regionalism has made good sense to some people as a means to moderate tension, and to others as a means to exacerbate it. One person's hegemony is another's imperialism. And still to others, regionalism is not so much a geopolitical Goldilocks' porridge as a superior position, attitude or form of global organization with its own mental map. As described in the following pages, this is well known. America has long existed as a distinct region in the minds of its inhabitants and outsiders, and it includes multiple subregions. The writer Joel Garreau, for example, has named nine in North America alone in his travelogue of the same title: "New England, The Foundry [the industrial Mid-Atlantic and Midwest], Dixie, the [Caribbean] Islands, Mexamerica, Ecotopia [Pacific Northwest], The Empty Quarter [the Rockies extending up to Alaska], the Breadbasket [the Great Plains extending from Winnipeg to Houston], Québec, and Aberrations [New York City, Washington, DC, Alaska and Hawaii], which do not fit within any of the nine."[14] One could draw similar maps further south: Amazonia, the Andean plateau, the Pampa, Patagonia, and so on. Doing so, as Garreau has admitted, serves to challenge existing political boundaries and to break them down into more meaningful parts; Garreau's readers, for example, will find distinctions among the fifty states of the US weaker after following his journey through his eyes and learning "the way North America really works." Just as some of the fiercest supporters of the European movement come from places like Catalonia, Flanders and the Mezzogiorno, one could ask whether an increasingly "glocal" (as in global plus local) America will come to embrace regionalism in a similar way.

However, first one must revisit some basics, starting with culture and ideology and then moving back again, in the final section, to politics.

# II

**W**hat then is the American, this new man?" asked the French expatriate J. Hector St. John de Crèvecœur, writing as the "American Farmer," in 1782. He was neither the first nor the last European to pose the question. Could one not ask it about any American, or, for that matter, anyone else? The question, "Who is a European?" for example, is heard perennially in Europe, whereas many non-Europeans would be surprised that this is up for debate. The reverse has generally been true for America. People throughout the hemisphere have tended to recognize themselves as Americans without question. One speaks here, however, mainly of European Americans; "Native" Americans do not regard themselves precisely in this way; others, notably African Americans, whose ancestors came to the hemisphere involuntarily, are even more equivocal, and they are the only major ethnic group in America that generally prefers a continental prefix to a national one. This has likely as much to do with geopolitical and other notions of Africa as it does with America, and is why, for example, a Chinese or Korean American may also use the term "Asian American" but few African Americans will use another, narrower term.

Most Americans, however, and especially most of European descent have traditionally defined their homeland in opposition to Europe, "less as precise geographical terms," the historian Daniel Boorstin has noted, "than as logical antitheses," and their homeland as "a happy deviant from an ancient European norm."[15] And so here one may see the first important part of the definition: the "American" in Crèvecœur's inquiry, and in many since, is primarily a transplanted European, yet also a "new" person for whom Europe exists as a reaffirmation of an alternate identity. He or she may be several generations removed from the "Old Country," but there is still this element in the territorial consciousness, even—as is increasingly the case in the United States and in other large countries like Brazil, Peru and Argentina, and throughout the Caribbean—if his or her ancestors came from other parts of the world besides Europe. Race and ethnicity are the *idées fixes* of America. They are never a simple matter when force coexists with mutability. Few people on earth, until relatively recently, were more self-conscious about pluralism in their societies yet have been, at the same time, so sensitive about widespread miscegenation. Few elsewhere have seen so high a proportion of their society made up of immigrants and few have been so keen to construct the layers of cultural solidarity— not only racial and ethnic but also religious and linguistic—in response. Thus the American is a "hybrid" person whose predominant literary culture originated in Europe but who has over the years become something else entirely. That culture derives, according to the Brazilian statesman, Joaquim Nabuco, from

> the sentiment of our own separate orbit, of an orbit absolutely detached from the European, in which Africa and Asia, not speaking of Australasia, are moving. With all our sympathy for Europe, conscious of all we owe to the European influx, products as we are of the overflow of the European races, doubting even that in our soil all the stems of European culture could ever produce the same fruits or the same flowers as in their native soil, we, however, elected to form a political system wholly unconnected with that of Europe.[16]

America may be unique among the regions in this respect. While all regions present a complex mixture of cultures—for there is no purely homogenous place on the earth—America is the only region that originated self-consciously at the onset of the modern era as almost entirely reconstructed: the "New World," both physically—since it was, as Columbian legend has it, "discovered" by accident—and spiritually, as European civilization's antipode and its regenerator.[17] Similar associations have been made to Asia in Orientalist discourse, to be sure, but America was cast as the only "virgin" territory where the paradox could flourish and the only one whose entire populations were depicted, and continue to be depicted, as living in a special land selected for a special purpose. Benjamin Franklin, "that typical child of the Enlightenment," for example,

> had prayed that "a thorough knowledge of the Rights of Man may pervade all nations of the earth, so that a philosopher may set foot anywhere on its surface and say 'This is my country.'" Early in the nineteenth century many Americans came to feel that the Western Hemisphere was the only part of the world which could answer Franklin's prayer. When they did so, the formation of the Western Hemisphere idea was complete.[18]

---

Despite the existence there of vast, populous civilizations—as well as empires in Mesoamerica and the Andean region of South America—the Europeans who invented America did so with the presumption of the *tabula rasa*, to be populated, or otherwise conquered and converted in order to make way for a new race and in the service of universal virtues or of the God who directed them there, as the case may be. "It is the business of *Americans*," said Noah Webster,

> to select the wisdom of all nations, as the basis of her constitutions— to avoid their errours—to prevent the introduction of foreign vices and corruptions and check the career of her own—to promote virtue and patriotism—to embellish and improve the sciences— to diffuse an uniformity and purity of *language*—to add superiour dignity to this infant Empire and to human nature.[19]

Others would describe how and why Americans transformed nature into glorifications of their "own" world: the poets Ercilla, Olmedo and Whitman, the philosophers Emerson and Zea, the novelists James Fenimore Cooper and Ricardo Rojas, the chroniclers Concolorcorvo, Garcilaso, Prescott and Parkman would describe the legends of the Americas as little different, really, in spirit than the best of the ancient epics. Tracing the fate of each and every one of these attempts here is less important, however, than realizing, again, that the underlying cultural and political basis of America is one of European ambivalence: about Europe and its place in the world; about the Old and the New; about the material and the spiritual; about the free and the enslaved; about the pure and the defiled; about the holy and the profane; about modernity itself. America cannot constitute a region otherwise; mere geography does not make it so. Rather, it is the idea (and ideal) of America as extension of, and alternative to, Europe that makes it distinct and coherent.

Returning to Crèvecœur's question, one should admit that most Americans do not think in these terms; yet many share an awareness of where they live. How do Americans perceive others as being less or more "like" themselves? Does a citizen of Canada have more in common—or feel that he or she has more in common—with one from Argentina or Mexico than with someone in China, England or Italy? There is no uniform answer. But if one takes seriously the idea of civilization, then acknowledging the existence of such affinities must be possible; and if they exist, then historicizing them must also be possible, even necessary. How best to do it? Neither an intellectual nor a political history of Americanism or even Americanization would suffice to answer the question because, as Arthur Whitaker has observed in his classic study of just one of its expressions—the Western Hemisphere idea—it has been at various times an ideological, political and economic project. One has to combine them into the history of a concept from the moment when Americans first asserted their political distinctiveness.

Historians of this moment—from roughly the last third of the 18th century to the end of the first third of the 19th, have come increasingly to understand the American independence movements as cultural as well as political events.[20] Nearly all of them were inter-elite struggles over power and authority, in Carl Becker's classic formulation, over who would rule at home as well as home rule. Although the revolutions in Spanish America came nearly a generation after the one in British America, and although their intellectual sources were somewhat different—the former having been inspired by the Scottish and French enlightenments, the latter by these but also by the Spanish contractualism of Vitoria and Suárez—all to one degree or another asserted a certain right of self-government for the subjects, later citizens, of America.[21] That such rights were "self-evident" within the framework of European empires struck few of the American patriots, later revolutionaries, as paradoxical: most regarded themselves as loyal imperial subjects whose rights as such were violated by flawed monarchs. Yet when they took the additional step and declared themselves republicans and their "revolutions" to be, at least for some, both anti-monarchical and in pursuit of an "independent" sovereignty, it was clear that they were in possession of an alternative territorial consciousness that called itself American. This is also to say that the various American wars of independence were, to some degree, parallel actions, each drawing at least some inspiration from the others and from the general spirit of the time. But understanding and characterizing that spirit is not easy, not least because so many contemporaries rejected the similarities. Whitaker has reminded us, for example, of John Adams' unkind reaction to the liberation plan advanced by Francisco de Miranda in 1797–98: "you might as well talk about establishing democracies among the birds, beasts, and fishes as among the Spanish American people."[22] Parallel perhaps; uniform, no.

Were the revolts genuine revolutions? The historian Lester Langley has written in his comparative study of the revolutionary age in the Americas that an answer to the question not only requires a consensus over the definition of a revolution but also an elaborate local understanding of each independence movement.[23] The British, French and Spanish empires differed markedly; that all three saw colonial populations declare and fight for independence during these decades, however, suggests at least some mutual influence. Influence was expressed in the newly "domestic" realm of politics, as local elites were forced to enlist others in their campaigns against colonial masters. "What made these upheavals distinctive," Langley has argued, was not only the demand from colonial elites within empires but the often reluctant choices they made in order to mobilize populations in their cause . . . in an age when political, economic, and social dynamics profoundly shook transatlantic empires, colonial elites wanted a different relationship with the home country and risked treason and war to achieve it. What they did not anticipate was the changes in their relationship with those who participated in these conflicts.[24]

That relationship, in turn, had a good deal to do with the nature of creole identity. It was similar to colonial identities across the world: just as latter 19th and 20th century descendants of Europeans in Africa and India called themselves, respectively, Africans and Indians—sometimes, for example, with an anglo- or another prefix, sometimes without—those in the Western Hemisphere came to call themselves Americans. What did it mean to be a creole? There was more to it than being a transplanted, even displaced, European. Creoles were not immigrants; they were born in the New World and looked to Europe as source of heritage, even sovereignty, with varying degrees of distance. Nor were they "amalgamated," that is to say, miscegenated, *mestizo*—despite the usage of "creole" in some parts of North America and the Caribbean (as applied mainly to food and language) in this sense. No, creole culture was an elite one. And the revolutions, such as they were, Langley concluded, were nearly all chaotic adaptations, some successful, others less so, to the reality of life and times in America among so many other groups of new Americans.[25]

The creole moment lasted only about a decade in each of the new republics. But the "successor nation" lived on.[26] In most cases it opened ground for nonelites to enter public life by way of a dramatic transformation of the local economy. The first third of the 19th century saw the boom of nation-building in the Americas: from the Hamiltonian "American system" in the US and then Jacksonian politics (seen, incidentally, as a competitor to the Hamiltonian vision, but in retrospect more as a complement, as sectionalism would give way to nationalism by way of popular democracy), to the proliferation of *caudillo* regimes throughout the Americas, including the United States. In retrospect, Andrew Jackson and Juan Manuel de Rosas differed less in style and inspiration than in their level of excess. These so-called men on horseback mobilized significant sectors of the free white population, and drew deeper racial and sectional lines of division in their societies while at the same time popularizing a nativist discourse that became dominant throughout the Americas by the middle of the century. They succeeded where Mariano Moreno, Francisco de Miranda, Andrés Bello, Simon Bolívar and other illustrious creoles failed: they reified the popular nation.[27]

Nationalism was a French import, and it was the post-revolutionary, Napoleonic, "modern" version that proved so durable in the Americas precisely because such "new" nations had emerged alongside new economies and powerful social hierarchies. As Tulio Halperín Donghi, Joyce Appleby and other historians have shown, this two sided process of *embourgeoisement* accomplished three goals: it reoriented—indeed, reconstructed almost in its entirety—the predominant economy away from the European, imperial pattern inward, so to speak, toward the so-called interior; it reshuffled—or, again, some would say, reconstructed— the socio-economic class system in most countries initially in order to reaffirm the power of creole elites while, to some extent, easing restrictions on social mobility to align those elites with a new, domestic bourgeoisie; and, finally, it promoted a messianic ideology alongside a national culture.[28] The process was not the same everywhere, and the distinctions and differences have stimulated long debates over causes and legacies. Many have resembled the strident determinism of Stanley and Barbara Stein (*The Colonial Heritage of Latin America*, 1970)—and have been based, again, on the notion of the American Janus, as a later critic has described it: a culture not "founded in rupture with its origins," but rather as a doomed attempt to "prolong Spanish ideals in the New World" and "the impossibility of choice" of "destiny" over "fate."[29] The real story was not so simple.

Earlier generations explained the consolidation of American nationalism by looking to the attributes of individuals and extrapolating from them the character of societies instead of the other way around, giving rise to Lord Acton's depiction of nationality as a voluntarist (and precarious) enterprise. This was the moment, one will recall, that Alexis de Tocqueville and Francis Grund wrote their treatises on the nature of the Americans in the United States; it was also the moment that, in opposition to the Rosas tyranny, exiles Juan Bautista Alberdi and Domingo Faustino Sarmiento formulated Argentine national ideology by way of an elaboration of the unique, modern character of the Argentine people—imagined, invented and constructed, to be sure, but having an essentialist mission nonetheless. The result of this nationalizing process was the setting into motion of a bitter contest for national power. By 1860 it had come to a head—in the United States, in the Colombian and Argentine Federations, etc.—where contending social, political, and ideological authorities came to see their "ways of life" under mortal threat. As with the earlier wars of independence, it is possible to view these civil struggles as essentially intramural or inter-elite contests. However, the insider/outsider dichotomy was now applied to the already extant nation and so was as much about how and by whom the nation would be ruled as it was about the standards by which it was ruled, and the moral future of its inhabitants. It spoke to the dichotomy that Sarmiento provided in his tract, *Facundo*, and that abolitionists in the United States employed in their depiction of the Southern slave power: Americans faced—again, as modern citizens of the New World, blessed by Providence to design and enact their future—a choice between civilization and barbarism: the mere existence of latter imperiled the former, only one could survive in this precious New World, and it was up to the people to choose, even with their blood. The problem for Sarmiento—as for others like the great Brazilian writer Euclides da Cunha who made much use of the dichotomy—was its translatability to multiple groups at once across the civilizational divide.

As it happened, unitary nationalists won nearly everywhere in the Americas, as they did, for that matter in Europe; by the early 1870s even fractious Germany and Italy had been unified under a centralized and powerful national regime. It has long been asserted that Bismarck and Lincoln had much in common in this respect, though they probably would have challenged the comparison (or at least Lincoln would have done; Bismarck was fond of Americans and of American comparisons even to the point of sounding out Washington on a German-American alliance.) They had technology, industry, economy, population and even the *Zeitgeist*, inasmuch as History makes use of such moods and forces, on their side.

All this meant that, by the last quarter of the 19th century, the quintessential American was the citizen of a national republic with a national economy, a national capital, and a national territory that was connected ever more closely by the railroad and the telegraph, and whose conationals were educated ever more rigorously in the virtues of the nation and the modern, American way of life. Even Brazilians, Canadians and Cubans—who remained subjects of European empires for most of the century—succumbed eventually to the mantra of civilization over barbarism, or "order and progress," as the Brazilian national motto puts it, against chaos amid torpor.

It is important to note here that, in spite of political upheavals in many countries in the mid-19th century, economic growth at home and a series of crises in Europe—the Irish potato famine and the revolutions of 1848—brought large numbers of immigrants to the Americas, beginning in these years and continuing until the first decades of the 20th century. Several countries—the United States, Canada, Argentina, and Brazil, as well as Mexico, Chile and Venezuela—saw the establishment of significant migrant societies in which the Old World/New World dichotomy was reaffirmed and magnified by successive generations of Americans who straddled the cultural boundaries of reinvention and commemoration. There never really was a true New World melting pot, as most historians now assert—it was something more like a kaleidoscope, the "trans-national America" once described so brilliantly by Randolph Bourne in his essay with that title (1916). The important element here is the re-inscribing, again, of the dichotomous nature of America. On the one hand, such migrants to the Americas had something in common, at least in their displacement, their "uprootedness," and most tended to realize this, on some level, when they encountered one another in their respective destinations. And yet in most of these countries, the children of these immigrants and indirectly the immigrants themselves were subjected to rigorous normal education stressing national particularities and destinies—as distinct not only from the nationalities these immigrants left behind but also, at times even more so, from those of neighboring nations and their intangible trappings—their new usable pasts, their unique characteristics, and their special destinies. By the end of the 19th century, that dichotomy had failed to mature into a New World dialectic; it came, in other words, to suffer from its inherent contradictions, with permanent novelty reaching its logical end in self-denial.[30] The material promise of America had begun to wane in some countries (particularly following economic crises in the early 1870s and 1890s), while the spiritual promise, to the extent that such a thing existed, had never quite blossomed. Why the failure?

One reason was that there still was no answer to Crèvecœur's question. Three quarters of a century since most of these nations gained their independence, nationalization had only just begun to take root, while the national image their intellectuals promoted had barely taken into account their place in the wider world. It was not so much that American nationalists were provincial—many were, following 19th century practice, well-read and for the most part cosmopolitan. Rather, it was that they had fallen in with a modern discourse that remained imperial, with America sitting on the periphery. Most of the world was still ruled by European empires; some of the new American republics, in fact, touted imperial-sounding missions—e.g., "empire for liberty," "manifest destiny," the "conquest of the wilderness," and so forth. Empires and imperialism did not necessarily contradict American nationalism, but they complicated the aim of demonstrating that America was both exceptional and superior in the world. And so, by the turn of the century, some American ideologues struck out in a different direction. There had to be more to American civilization than met the eye: it must amount to something greater than all that land, and something better than all those canals, railroads, factories, farms, towns, cities, inventions and freedoms. No, America also had a special soul.

The problem was that the soul proved to be divisible as well. In the United States romantics like Emerson and Whitman had already given a voice to the spiritual impulse; by the end of the century it had become a literary commonplace, as elaborated in T. J. Jackson Lears' *No Place of*

*Grace.* So, too, in Latin America, except there it would soon acquire a distinct, negative hue. This came with the publication, in 1900, of the book *Ariel*, by the Uruguayan writer José Enrique Rodó. Rodó is not regarded today as an especially remarkable writer, although he was by contemporaries. *Ariel* was just one of those books that came along at exactly the right time, making the author famous throughout the Spanish-speaking world and establishing an ideology: *Arielismo.* The story was dedicated to the "youth of America" and set in a classroom where a teacher, a rendition of Shakespeare's Prospero with the same name, instructs his students to avoid imitating the "Nordomania" of Caliban. *Ariel* was an allegory of the modern world embodied by the American continent. The materialistic North was at war with the spiritual South; the former was driven by avarice, the latter by virtue; the North American was flawed, corrupted, by the gospel of wealth; the Latin American was, potentially, a figure of perfection. Rodó did not attack the United States outright; he did not attack its existence, nor did he, at least at this stage in his career, condemn it for its actions elsewhere in the hemisphere. His preoccupation rather was with the temptation posed by materialism to the spiritual life of *his* American people.[31] In essence, he flipped Sarmiento's distinction on its head: the civilized United States presented a false alternative to barbarism, in some ways even more barbaric than all it stood against in the name of progress.[32]

The political setting for *Arielismo* is important to bear in mind: its juxtaposition of the material and the spiritual had as much to do with turn-of-the-century America as with a reaction to the defeat of the Spanish Empire, which coincided with the rise to prominence of a group of Latin American writers and artists who came to call themselves modernists and who, according to the scholar Jean Franco, were the "first generation of professional writers in Spanish America."[33] They joined an artistic and spiritual revolt with an ideological and political one; the artist had to separate himself from society in order to redeem it. Although much of Latin America had been on the side of the Cuban revolt against the Spanish, few there rushed to ally themselves with the United States as the self-appointed liberator and defender. It did not take long for leading literary figures like Rodó; the Nicaraguan poet, Rubén Darío; and, above all, the Cuban patriot, poet and journalist, José Martí, whose US-based writings already had revealed him as a kind of anti-Tocqueville, to denounce the *yanqui* usurpation of the Cuban (i.e., American) revolution. Their 1898-style "anti-Americanism" (as in anti-US) would reverberate for at least another century in Latin America, reaching its apex from the late 1950s to the mid-1970s and led by the heirs to that conflict, notably Fidel Castro, the illegitimate son of a Spanish soldier. Here is Darío, in "To Roosevelt" (1904):

But our own America, which has had poets
since the ancient times of Nezahualcóyotl;
which preserved the footprints of great Bacchus,
and learned the Panic alphabet once,
and consulted the stars, which also knew Atlantis
(whose name comes ringing down to us in Plato)
and has lived, since the earliest moments of its life,
in time, in fire, in fragrance, and in love—
the America of Moctezuma and Atahualpa,
the aromatic America of Columbus,
Catholic America, Spanish America,
the America where noble Cuauhtémoc said:
"I am not on a bed of roses"—our America,
trembling with hurricanes, trembling with Love:
O men with Saxon eyes and barbarous souls,
our America lives. And dreams. And loves.
And it is the daughter of the Sun. Be careful.
Long live Spanish America!
A thousand cubs of the Spanish lion are roaming free.
Roosevelt, you must become, by God's own will,
the deadly Rifleman and the dreadful Hunter
before you can clutch us in your iron claws.
And though you have everything, you are lacking in one thing:
    God![34]

And Martí (1889):

> And how can one fail to remember, for the glory of those who
> have known how to conquer, in spite of them, the confused
> and bloodsoaked origins of Our America, although the faithful
> memory (more necessary now than ever) may be stained with
> untimely senility by the one whom the light of our glory—the
> glory of our independence—had hindered in the work of com-
> promising or demeaning that America of ours? North America
> was born of the plow, Spanish America of the bulldog. A fa-
> natical war took from the poetry of his aerial palaces the Moor
> weakened by his riches; and the remaining soldiers, reared to
> heresy on hate and sour wine and equipped with suits of ar-
> mor and arquebuses, rushed upon the Indian protected by his
> breastplate of cotton. . . . Where is America going, and who
> will unite her and be her guide? Alone and as one people she
> is rising. Alone she is fighting. Alone she will win. . . . And we

have transformed all this venom into sap! Never was there such a precocious, persevering, and generous people born out of so much opposition and unhappiness. We were a den of iniquity and we are beginning to be a crucible.[35]

The latitudinal juxtaposition was not confined to the Americas; it is found in almost every other part of the world, not least in Europe, where Rodó's division between the North and the South could just as easily apply to a number of European nations on either side of the Alps. As any reader of Lears' book will know, the antimaterialist, or antimodern (as he has called it) reaction was pronounced in the United States as well. Darío was not the only one who regarded some North Americans as "buffaloes with their silver teeth . . . cyclopses, eaters of raw meat, bestial blacksmiths, inhabitants of houses of mastodons." It is important to recall, moreover, that "it was in New York that Martí began to change the language of Latin American Spanish, shifting away from what he termed metaphors replete with 'suffering and victimhood,' expressions like 'to write our history with blood,' toward descriptions and structures that rely on demonstrative logic."[36]

In the wider American setting, however, the longitudinal (old versus new) dichotomy superimposed itself upon the latitudinal one so that there emerged something like a four way contest in which the spiritual "South" and the material "North" vied for the messianic mantle of the New World. Juxtaposing the "civilization of the spirit" with the "civilization of the machine" ("the star-spangled Babylon") resulted not only from intellectual opportunism but also from complicated reactions to modernity that were to an extent universal. "American civilization," was just "one of the main mythical metaphors, which was perceived ambivalently, as a phenomenon both terrifying and fascinating."[37] No wonder that some Latin Americans blurred the longitudinal contrast so much that they came to argue that the Old World really was not so bad after all; indeed, according to this view, one of the virtues of Latin American culture was that it sought to preserve, and even improve upon, the best of European (although primarily Mediterranean) civilization as a way of resisting a more immediate threat, US power.[38] Martí would thus vary Sarmiento's distinction as not one between civilization and barbarism *per se* but between false erudition and nature.

One will recall that many of the Latin American modernists were ardent Francophiles as would be later generations: a long list of writers and artists—from Vicente Huidobro, Alejo Carpentier, César Vallejo and César Moro to José Lezama Lima and Julio Cortazar—found their inspiration, and in many cases their livelihood, in France, where intellectuals had long distinguished their brand of modernity and its global value from that of nominal Anglo-Saxons. Recall too that "Latin" America, according to one standard account, was a recent invention resulting from the French invasion of Mexico and the attempt by Napoleon III to create a Catholic, New World Empire.[39] The older generation of nationalists—Sarmiento, for example—resisted that orientation, having as his model the United States of America as both material and spiritual guide. (Sarmiento had spent time in the US but, unlike Martí, advertised an ideal view of it, even taking to calling himself *"Franklincito"*). The next generation came to see itself at the center of a West in dialogue with itself, both longitudinally and latitudinally, rather than as the inheritor or redeemer of an obsolescent world. What should properly be called "Ibero-America" (although that term excludes much of the Caribbean) may be thought of, following Rodó, as a mirror image of North America and a counterpoint to the rational, the liberal and the materialist, but in other ways, as its own unique civilization, not merely a reflection or variation on something else.[40]

Cultural idealism became more pronounced at the turn of the century for reasons besides the Spanish-American war. There was the related campaign to establish and promote the United States as a world power, and the reaction to it, particularly among US "anti-imperialists" who warned of the end of the republic and the loss of what had become a cherished American ideal. It did not draw so clear a line between republicanism and imperialism—in fact the two were consistent in most cases—but by now the latter ideology had been transformed by wartime jingoism into an objectionable brand of colonialism.

The war brought the establishment of US protectorates in Cuba, Puerto Rico and the Philippines, thereby stretching the American mental map all the way to Asia and placing the United States in a direct strategic position vis-à-vis Japan and China. Anti-imperialists took their stand but did not prevent the United States from eventually entering another war, the First World War, with the rationale of safeguarding the Western Hemisphere from conflict—as trafficked by marauding German submarines that menaced life and treasure on the Atlantic, and by purported German meddling in the domestic and regional affairs of American states.

The general effect of the First World War upon America, particularly Latin America, was to constrain ties with the Old World in limiting British and French investment, and making Latin American markets more attractive to US competition.[41] The interwar years also saw the deeper economic involvement of the United States in the Europe and the resumed entanglement of Europe in world politics. By the middle of the 1930s, few could claim plausibly that the global depression did not result from the flawed aftermath of the war, while the populist, state-led reactions had much in common. Leadership styles resurrected some aspects of the previous century's *caudillo* politics, now updated in the manner of Franco and Mussolini. Even the austere architecture of the period looked much the same from capital to capital.[42]

But what of America and Americanism? Populism echoed in the literary culture. These decades also saw the rise of regionalism throughout the world, which advertised itself in some cases as a counterweight to nationalism but in other cases seemed like just another version of it, a super- or "macronationalism."[43] Globalism, at least in the dressing of the League of Nations, was rated a failure alongside capitalism; regional "autarky" and regional politics were promoted to varying degrees worldwide as the more responsible and more responsive basis for world order.[44] Several trends, in fact, complemented one another. In addition to a revised passion for regionalism among such figures as Richard von Coudenhove-Kalergi, Aristide Briand and Jean Monnet, there was the popularization of Spenglerian meditations on the success or failure of "civilizations."[45] The leading historian of the United States, Charles Beard, who had made a name for himself as a mildly Marxian debunker of nationalist myths, wrote (together with his wife, Mary) the four-volume *Rise of American Civilization* around this time. Few major North American writers have given so delicate a combination of self-absorption and critique, ostensibly progressive but bordering at times on the cynical. (They termed Spengler's contribution "a massive pile of pretentious erudition" and went on to quote Freud's description of American civilization as "a miscarriage").[46] Yet the Beards immersed themselves in the sea of collective virtue. Their writing is a cross between that of Toynbee, Brooks Adams, Walt Whitman, John Dos Passos, and perhaps Jean Giono or Ernst Jünger, as though the reader ought to wonder whether he or she is meant to have a heuristic or a spiritual experience when reading it. Indeed, this latter quality continued to animate regionalism during the interwar years in America. Echoing Rodó, Charles Beard recalled,

> 'Sir, the Spirit of Continental Independence, the Genius of American Liberty, which in earlier times tried her infant voice in the halls and on the hills of New England, utters it now, with power that seems to wake the dead, on the plains of Mexico and along the sides of the Andes.' With this gorgeous flourish the great Daniel Webster greeted the new independent republics of Latin America more than a hundred years ago. Since that time . . . something significant has happened. If our grand experiment in freedom once inspired the followers of Benito Juarez to noble emulation, it seems that the oblations now poured out by President Coolidge on the altar of Liberty leave President Calles cold and dubious.

. . . If American merchants, masters of finance and captains of industry manage to wring all they want from the Mexican government by mere economic pressure and the rest of us—pure in heart—get all the oil, copper and hemp we need, should American laborers, humanitarians, churchmen and plain people imagine they see any stains on their hemp, copper and coupons or in their gasoline? Evidently the business is not simple. . . . [47]

Beard was a Midwesterner; his Americanism was of the smaller variety (as in Little England, *Kleindeutschland* or *patria chica*); and his romanticism extended inward toward socioeconomic, political and cultural improvement. He became an isolationist and a bitter opponent of the Roosevelt administration, penning one of his most strident books, *The Open Door at Home*.

His brand of romanticism, however, was neither exclusive to the American Midwest nor so blatantly nationalistic. A similar romantic was the writer Waldo Frank. Frank grew up in New York City and was a member of that city's literary *jeunesse dorée* of the first decades of the 20th century. He may have been cursed by too much early success, and so became a contrarian on a mission, determined to find his promised land, which, as a child, he had called "Waldea." The First World War drove Frank, like Beard, to nativism: his *Our America*, published in 1919, was similar in substance to the Beards' later histories, although more histrionic. Like some contemporaries, Frank migrated to France, but abandoned it for Spain. This, combined with a fascination with Latin America that he had acquired from exiles he met in Paris, drew Frank to "rediscover" the Western Hemisphere, becoming one of the most devoted hispanophiles and exponents of New World messianism in the English language.[48]

Like his contemporary, the Mexican writer José Vasconcelos and author of *La raza cósmica*, America to Frank was in search of a "dynamic heritage" that would "comman[d] profound emotional legitimacy" from all its parts: the "three Americas" (in this case, English, Spanish and Portuguese) ought to merge into a single America, uniting their component races—the Anglo-Saxon, the Hispanic, the Indian, and the African—into a single "island" civilization (an echo of *Ariel*) while displacing the "inward enemy": a "continental psychology" that leaves little room for anything besides "a feeling of invulnerability" from being "strong in defense, lethargic in attack." By contrast, "[t]he people that feels itself an island, because it is vulnerable, becomes aggressive."[49] This did not have to become a liability. The island mentality would serve, according to Frank, to unite art and life in order to guarantee the expression of the "whole man," which America lacked.[50]

Frank, in other words, suffered from the same ambivalence about the Old World. Many, perhaps most, people in the Americas knew very little about their putative neighbors; many still looked toward Europe as the world's political and cultural "center," and not to themselves. Regionalism needed a more powerful force to inspire and persuade adherents to believe and to feel that they had more in common with one another than with anyone from any other part of the world.

This did not happen in the Americas for two reasons. The first was the persistent gap in regional familiarity, overcome somewhat by travel, education and exchange but not exclusive to this region. The second was the ascent of Atlanticism. This was another old concept that was, in the helpful distinction of the historian David Armitage, as much cisatlantic as it was circumatlantic and transatlantic.[51] That is to say, the Atlantic was a lake (or pond, some would say) as well as a river and an ocean.

However, Atlanticism referred mainly to the North Atlantic. Nearly everything below the equator was auxiliary.[52] Leading Atlanticists like the journalists Walter Lippmann, who coined the term "Atlantic Community," and Clarence Streit gave almost no place of prominence to Latin America, apart from the Caribbean and Eastern Brazil, in their cartography; the rest of South America, as Henry Kissinger later quipped, might as well be little more than a dagger pointed at the heart of Antarctica. Both Lippmann and Streit, incidentally, were disappointed Wilsonians—Lippmann as one of Wilson's aides who subsequently resigned from the Paris Peace Commission, and Streit as a newspaper correspondent in Geneva. According to them the regional idea was necessary and more practical than the alternatives. Yet for his Atlantic union, Streit favored reviving—and not at all ironically—the name Atlantis, which was proposed to him by the diplomat William Bullitt, another of Lippmann's former comrades in arms at Paris. Whether based upon a union or a community (the two blur in practice), this version of Atlanticism was meant to be a political, ideological, cultural and economic rendition of the North Atlantic area. Some versions saw it spreading gradually to the East and to the South, but were unenthusiastic about a deliberate expansion in these directions, just as the early visionaries of Europeanism—particularly Jean Monnet, who disliked the idea of his community's enlargement beyond the United Kingdom, even to Scandinavia—insisted that viability meant clear limits. Atlanticists insisted similarly—though with a different map at hand—that the union of North Atlantic democracies was critical for the survival of the West and the political culture it had come to champion. Muddling the composition of the community meant diluting or paralyzing the fulfillment of its mission. "Pan-America seems to me," wrote Streit, "to be . . . partly a hangover from the old belief (so old that one might even call it the cave-man belief) that land unites men, and water separates them."[53] The North Atlantic was too important a region to get wrong, whereas in most of the Americas, in Streit's view, governments had been too immature, weak or divided to present a case for supplanting, or conceiving a union, with Europe:"[I]t was dangerous too to treat these republics on the same basis as the autocracies of the Old World." Hence the Monroe Doctrine, a "middle course, still exceedingly bold."[54]

The Atlantic union/community had a clear imperative and a ready supply of will and talent. It was meant to serve as a kind of nucleus (Streit used that term) and also as an antidote to the "germ" of "absolute nationalism" everywhere. Since it would be impolitic to admit just one or two Latin American democracies to the union, Streit concluded that it simply would be best to leave them all out. Lippmann took exclusion in a different direction, depicting Latin America in negative terms as a potential back door for threatening "the American position" but possessing little to offer otherwise. His American defense perimeter did include all of North and South America in order to preserve control of the Natal to Dakar line for military reasons. But that was the extent of it.[55]

The geostrategic approach to the Americas in fact turned the Monroe Doctrine inside out; meant to insulate the hemisphere from more intensive European intervention, it came, according to Lippmann, to "guarante[e] us a free hand as against Europe and Asia," while "the dis-union of the Latin-American states assures us a free hand as against them."[56] During the Second World War, the United States and its allies in the Americas made much of the "Hemisphere of Peace," partly to reassure isolationists at home, but also to counterpoise America as a source of stability and strength to war-ravaged Europe and Asia. Rather than refocusing inward in order to dissuade outside powers from intervention, as Beard and the isolationists had urged, it sought instead to project strength outward. This was the culture in reserve, in Franklin Roosevelt's depiction (suggested to him, reportedly, by Monnet) of the United States: the "arsenal of democracy." It did not stand apart from Europe or Asia but existed instead as an engine and a beacon for them and the rest of the world.

That did little for the cause of Americanism *per se*. Without a transatlantic mission, and continuing to set itself apart from Europe, it did not have much to offer. It was that mission—rediscovered by a now hegemonic United States—that dominated the remainder of the 20th century.

The cultural question remained unresolved. The geographer Carl Sauer once taught (with reference to Mesoamerica) that political borders eventually shift or are redefined by demography as well as culture. To date this has not happened in the Americas to the degree that it did in the 19th century, in contrast to what has taken place in other continents since 1945. Politically the hemisphere is "settled" but culturally it is far from it. The difficulty comes in attempting to disaggregate cultural shifts from wider ones such as globalization. How do most Americans define themselves globally? With today's Europeans, one generally hears a straightforward nomenclature: within Europe, people tend to say, I am French, Italian, German, Dutch, and so forth. Only when Europeans travel to other regions do they say they are "European," with a few minor exceptions, e.g., elderly Greeks or an even smaller number of Britons who still say they are going "to Europe" when they visit Paris. But few Brazilians or Canadians or Paraguayans call themselves Americans when traveling outside the Western Hemisphere. Only citizens of the United States do. There are no equivalent Erasmus-style exchange programs in the Americas, and while Latin Americans tend to gravitate toward North America for economic opportunity, the same has yet to happen in reverse, although many more people are multilingual. North Americans still look to Europe, and increasingly to Asia, when they strike out in the world. Today's Che Guevaras of the Americas—the romantics who journey to or from Tierra del Fuego—are rarities; even Guevara divided his America in two.

It has been said that geographic "propinquity . . . is an unescapable fact."[57] Still, Americanism has made sense mostly on a particular, subjective map. Streit had a point. It takes about 12 hours to fly from New York to Buenos Aires; it takes about half the time to fly across the Atlantic to London on a good day. The Caribbean—once known as the American Mediterranean—is much more proximate, and neighborhoods of some cities in the United States—New York, Miami, Houston, et al—might as well be Caribbean capitals. But to compare the cultures and worldviews of, say, a Mexican and a Uruguayan, or of a citizen of Montreal with one from Cuzco, is obviously another matter. What do they really have in common? If it is possible to generalize at all, how can any one cultural affinity they share be said to supplant any other? Over two centuries since Crèvecœur asked his question about only one part of the hemisphere, there is still no answer.

# III

The cultural and intellectual evolution of the Americas has not coincided neatly with its political, economic and institutional development. The latter at times advanced vis-à-vis Europe; at other moments it halted or saw reversals in the face of nationalist or local reactions. Most of it, however, was animated by, or at least reflected, cultural assumptions and aims.

Apart from measures designed to consolidate colonial rule at various points during the 17th and 18th centuries, the first well known regional project was Bolívar's reputed plan to unite the Americas. It included only Spanish America and, unfortunately in the eyes of later *bolivarianos*, was highly Anglophile. The idea essentially was to create a regional bloc, allied with the British, to offset or balance Spanish and French influence elsewhere in the Western Hemisphere. Bolívar himself understood its limits: "It is a grandiose idea to think of consolidating the New World into a single nation," he wrote in his Jamaica letter of 1815, "united by pacts into a single bond."

> It is reasoned that, as these parts have a common origin, language, customs, and religion, they ought to have a single government to permit the newly formed states to unite in a confederation. But this is not possible. Actually, America is separated by climatic differences, geographic diversity, conflicting interests, and dissimilar characteristics. How beautiful it would be if the Isthmus of Panamá could be for us what the Isthmus of Corinth was for the Greeks! Would to God that some day we may have the good fortune to convene there an august assembly of representatives of republics, kingdoms, and empires to deliberate upon the high interests of peace and war with the nations of the other three-quarters of the globe. This type of organization may come to pass in some happier period of our regeneration. But any other plan, such as that of Abbé St. Pierre, who in laudable delirium conceived the idea of assembling a European congress to decide the fate and interests of those nations, would be meaningless.[58]

As it happened, Bolívar inspired several regionalisms of a smaller dimension in the 1830s: the Peru-Bolivian Confederation, for example, and the Federal Republic of Central America. Though none would last, the idea would resurface again: for example, with the 1856 Continental Treaty between Chile, Peru and Ecuador; with Juan Ortega Rubio's call in 1917 for an Ibero-American union; and with Mercosur and similar trade blocs in the late 20th and early 21st centuries.[59]

Bolívar's vision may have suffered most from poor timing. His realization that the security and prosperity of the new American nations depended much upon the attitude of the British was an accurate one; yet it failed to accommodate the presence and potential power of the United States, whose leaders had come to similar conclusions about both Britain and the Western Hemisphere, only in reverse. "One of the chief victims of the war of 1812 was the Latin American policy of the United States," Whitaker has observed. The United States was desperate to keep Spain from helping the British, given sensitivities in the Floridas, which remained under Spanish rule, and subsequently, "g[ave] the British an almost entirely free hand in consolidating their political and economic influence in Latin America." But by now the US faced south, not just west, "towards Latin America, and there, not unexpectedly, found itself face to face with Europe again"[60]

This was the basis for the aforementioned "doctrine" of President James Monroe. It built upon earlier ideas, notably those of Thomas Jefferson, was formulated by the secretary of state, John Quincy Adams, and was issued in 1823 in order to prevent the effort by British foreign secretary and later prime minister, George Canning (the man who contributed the famous line, "I called the New World into existence, to redress the balance of the Old") to devise a joint alliance.[61] Adams decided to stand alone and draw the line on his side of the Atlantic. Canning then withdrew the proposal. What later came to be called the Monroe Doctrine, again, was not regionalist in the strict sense: it was more anticolonial than Americanist *per se*; and it was not enforceable. The 20th century US diplomat, William Castle, later described it aptly as a "traffic stop signal for foreign nations with expansionist ideas."[62] At the time it merely stated a preference. And, as Ernest May has recounted in his history of its origins, it had a domestic rationale from the presidential election of 1824, a story too complicated to tell here.[63] Over the decades, however—or at least by 1898—it came to acquire its popular connotation as the protector and enforcer of power in the Western Hemisphere.[64] As a symbol of American solidarity, for better or worse (for it has had as many critics as supporters), however, the Monroe Doctrine amounts to little more than an example of *post hoc ergo propter hoc*. In truth, the new states of Latin America nearly all looked to Britain, and to the British navy, as the guarantor of their independence; and the United States, which had little to offer them, also took advantage of the very same "free security" the British provided after 1815.

The Monroe Doctrine did not embody regionalism in the usual sense: its emphasis was primarily negative, even if it "marked the emergence of a new policy, namely a special policy towards Latin America which was based on different principles from the policy of the United States toward the rest of the world."[65] Adams, once he became president, may have gone on to consider more proactive elements of cooperation among the American republics, but they were not written into the policy, or into later interpretations until the very end of the 19th century. Some enthusiasts may have wanted to see the "Monroe Doctrine and the Pan-American Doctrine as two rivers which, having flowed a long way in the same direction but in separate channels, finally merge in one vast overwhelming stream," but that would take some time to happen, if ever.[66]

The prospect was hindered by the 1826 Panama Congress—the first of its kind in the hemisphere—and by most accounts a disaster. "The marriage of the two Americas ended in divorce before there was a honeymoon," was Whitaker's verdict.[67] The delegates from the United States in fact never arrived in time, a failure that was reciprocated the following year at Mexico when others were kept waiting for several of their South American counterparts, who never came.[68]

More meetings were held but "hemispherism went into a coma" for the remainder of the 19th century.[69] The vogue of Young Americanism in the United States, which called for the spread of Jacksonian democracy to Europe, had little to do with regionalism. There was also a similar, romantic literary movement of the same name, but it also was nationalistic. The *caudillo* tyrannies, followed by the struggles between unionists and federalists or confederalists, took up the remaining years of a very nationalist century. Some additional regional thinking took place—e.g., the so-called purple dream among a number of Southerners in the United States which suggested the spread of the plantation economy southward to Mexico and beyond; the periodic threat by Northerners there to annex parts of Canada; and the interstate conflicts in South America between 1865–70 and again in 1879 that featured some regionalist rhetoric. But it was only in the 1880s that a regionalist *project* resurfaced, not from Latin America but this time from the United States.

Credit went to the politician James Blaine and several like-minded publicists: William Eleroy Curtis, Hinton Helper, and a former US minister in Peru, Francis Thomas.[70] With the United States having begun its global "take-off" there was pressure to secure new markets for export and investment. A push toward Latin America seemed natural, as was the pressure exerted upon Latin American governments to grant favorable terms, even (or especially) at the expense of foreign, namely British, interests. What was less obvious was the regionalist import of Blaine's project. In articulating a connection between a regional trading bloc and solidarity in the hemisphere, he claimed to have found a formula for preserving peace and harmony while gaining commercial leverage over European rivals. It is not otherwise clear where or why Blaine acquired his idea. Political ambition probably had something to do with it: "Blaine from Maine" had the reputation of being one of the most ambitious men in public life.[71] Anyhow, his plan struck a chord that was louder than earlier, similar proposals by fellow North Americans like Henry Clay and Stephen Douglas, or those by the Argentine Juan Bautista Alberdi, who called for a "practical Pan-Americanism" and a hemispheric law based on liberty, free trade, and the balance of power; or by the Colombian José María Torres Caicedo and the Chilean Pedro Félix Vicuña.[72]

Yet, Blaine's project was nearly ended by the assassination of President James Garfield in 1881. Blaine lost his position as secretary of state, and his successor cancelled the resumption of the pan-American conference, rescinding all the invitations. But, as luck would have it, Blaine got another chance; another Republican was elected president a few years later and reappointed him. The conference took place in Washington at the end of 1889, and resulted in proposals for a pan-American customs union with standardized customs regulations and laws for copyright and trademark, a pan-American railway and improvements in steamship service, an arbitration union, a common silver currency and, finally, a commercial bureau that evolved into the Pan-American Union, forerunner of the OAS.

The conference was seen critically in some quarters.[73] The future Argentine president, Roque Sáenz Peña, for example, asserted, "What I lack is not love for America, but suspicion and ingratitude towards Europe. I cannot forget that in Europe are Spain, our mother; Italy, our friend; and France, our elder sister." Instead of "America for Americans," he suggested, one ought to say "America for all mankind."[74] Yet the coincidence of the conference with the United States' new proactivity and the emerging international law movement made it possible for turn-of-the-century internationalism to lay claim to an Americanist origin. Harvard's president Charles W. Eliot summarized it in five contributions of America to the world—one presumes he meant the United States but, as the passage was quoted by Joaquim Nabuco, it also could apply to the rest of America: "substitution of discussion and arbitration for war as the means of settling disputes between nations; second, the widest religious toleration; third, manhood suffrage; fourth, the demonstration of the fitness of a great variety of races for political freedom; fifth, the diffusion of material well-being among the population."[75] Thus as a commercial, even political, initiative, Blaine's pan-Americanism planted a seed that would, by some accounts, flourish over the course of the next century, even if it never became the "great Banyan tree" with a US trunk as it was later described by William Jennings Bryan.[76] It did not live up to his hopes of issuing a new creed based on "our common fate as inhabitants of the New World" with "like sympathies" and "like duties."[77] But it left a lasting symbol, perhaps a bit more than a "tissue of hopeful words."[78] No longer were nationalism and regionalism mutually exclusive tendencies in the Western hemisphere.

Pan-Americanism never really took root as a political force, however. It was "fictitious" to some degree and lacked the "faith and trust [that] have a way of transforming fiction into fact." "America for the Americans," according to the historian of nationalism, Carlton Hayes was a "dichotomy" bred from "ignorance," "self-centered absorption in local or sectional concerns, and of nationalist propaganda." Moreover, he later wrote, "[w]e used to know that we were Europeans as well as Americans, that we were not Indians or a people miraculously sprung from virgin forests like the primitive Germans described by Tacitus, but modern Europeans living in America on a frontier of Europe." For its part, "Latin America is more closely related, in culture and outlook, with Latin Europe than with the United States." Given the distribution of global power, pan-Americanism would only be viable if it were embedded somehow in a larger Western community; otherwise it did not make much political sense.[79]

In the meantime, there came a new imperialist move in the name of such a (re)distribution.. Theodore Roosevelt not only conspired in the 1898 war but also, once he became the US president, helped to foment a revolution in Panama with the aim of securing title to the Isthmus in order to build a canal, which his country presently did. The canal took another decade or so to be completed, by which point Woodrow Wilson was president, and the Caribbean—formerly a strategic *cul-de-sac*, to use Mahanian language—became an important bridge between the Atlantic and the Pacific, on a par, Wilson said, with the Turkish conquest of Constantinople in "switch[ing] the route of trade around" and seeing to it that his country "ceased to be a provincial Nation."[80] Bridges and *culs-de-sac* seemed to require a more assertive diplomacy, and along with it, another declaration of national superiority.

Roosevelt's 1904 corollary to the Monroe Doctrine stipulating a free hand to intervene in Latin America was blatantly imperialistic and was seen to be so. For his part, Wilson, who began office by pledging to respect his country's neighbors, did precisely the opposite, at least according to most of them, having intervened militarily in the Caribbean and in Mexico more than any of his recent predecessors. Wilson's determination—notoriously professed by him, to teach Latin Americans "to elect good men"—did not advance the cause of inter-American harmony. Mark Gilderhus, in his monograph on the subject, has described the impulse more charitably as aiding "the ongoing efforts of the United States to manage the affairs of the western hemisphere and to bestow more orderly and predictable structures upon its relations with the countries of Latin America."[81] Again, one person's hegemony was another's *imperialismo*. The contrast was captured well by the Argentine socialist Manuel Ugarte in an open letter to Wilson:

> You represent a civilization that was born from a choice, that substituted, as a point of departure, moral law for brute force, that flowered in the warmth of our ideals, like a reaction against the old errors of the world; and it would not be logical that you should commit, against us, assaults as grievous as those that Europe has committed in Asia and in Africa, because if you behave in that way, you would declare that your greatest, most illustrious predecessors were mistaken when they claimed to establish a new nation based on justice, and you would instead proclaim the bankruptcy of human perfection and of God's will.[82]

Both forms of regional penetration were affected by the war in Europe, which drew attention away from the hemisphere, gaining for the Mexicans a respite when the US General John Pershing's troops were withdrawn from its northern border where they had been chasing Pancho Villa, so they could be sent to fight in France. Wilson's efforts to see passage of the Pan American Pact—which sought the potential to create a kind of "American league" that, in the words of Eliot, might be "a suggestive precedent for a European League to keep the peace of Europe"—would meanwhile reckon even worse than the one at Geneva.[83]

The decade after the war, as noted, brought large quantities of US investment to Latin America and a growing number of Latin American immigrants to the United States; migrants from the Western Hemisphere were exempted from the restrictive immigration legislation that prohibited all but a tiny number from elsewhere. What had been called "dollar diplomacy" at the beginning of the century had resumed but its tone had changed: gone were the bluster and hypocrisy of the Roosevelt and Wilson administrations. The more that North, Central and South Americans lived and worked side by side, the more familiar their interaction generally became. There were occasional ruptures but these were better handled. When the Calles administration in Mexico, for example, nationalized much of the economy, including US-owned oil properties, President Calvin Coolidge sent Dwight Morrow, a clever banker from the House of Morgan, there as the new ambassador. Morrow charmed many Mexicans and breathed new life into what had been a very rough relationship for over a century. "They quite obviously prefer one Morrow in Mexico City to ten Sandinos in the bush," noted Walter Lippmann, referring to the Nicaraguan rebel.[84]

That smile on the face of American diplomacy would culminate in the 1930s with the Good Neighbor Policy. It was promoted by the Franklin Roosevelt administration as an alternative to what had come before, but it had already been set into motion by the previous two Republican presidents, particularly Herbert Hoover, who took a special interest in several Latin American countries and had made an earlier tour there in 1928. The Good Neighbor Policy brought important dividends. Firstly, in renouncing the policy of military intervention (with the aim of meddling in the politics of any other country although not to protect US citizens or property), it brought the United States' stance toward Latin America into line with Wilsonian principles, thereby placing American nationalism and regionalism on the same progressive side, in notable contrast to the US stance in Asia and Europe in the 1930s, and in a way resurrecting Blaine's policy.[85] Next, in reaffirming the sovereignty of the nations of the hemisphere, it advanced the idea of a community of equal members. The record was mixed in practice. But the language and tone of regionalism had changed for the better.

Historians do not agree on whether the era of good feelings in the Americas was prolonged or undercut by the demands of the Second World War and the Cold War. Although some of its language would survive—notably in the Alliance for Progress of the 1960s—the premises changed. The world was bifurcated politically and ideologically, and the United States had become leader of one camp. Its American neighbors once again appeared likely prey for "back door" subterfuge by outside powers as they had off and on since the days of Monroe. Nazis were hunted as well as sheltered throughout Latin America during the war; independent minded leaders like Perón prolonged the benefits of fence-sitting for as long as they could while tweaking the nose of the United States; leftists throughout the hemisphere did the same once it became clear that the Soviet Union would survive the war and become even more powerful, albeit halfway across the world.

The Cold War did not take long to arrive in America, and geopolitics came back into fashion. The Rio Pact was augmented by the Treaty of Bogota in 1948; that same year saw the rebranding of the Pan-American Union as the OAS. The *Bogotazo*, a loud revolt that drew many young rebels from throughout Latin America—including a Cuban law student called Fidel Castro—also took place in 1948 following the assassination of the Colombian president. The same Castro became a household name a decade later when he led a popular revolution in Cuba against the US-allied dictatorship of Fulgencio Batista. The legacy of 1898 and its anti-*yanqui* passions were rechristened with the ideology of the Cold War, and Castro and his comrades were quick to proclaim themselves Communists at war with capitalists and imperialists. For their troubles they gained the ostensibly unflinching support of the Soviet Union.

In response came the aforementioned Alliance for Progress—a kind of hybrid Marshall Plan/New Deal-style development initiative. America was again divided, although just as much internally within each nation as between North and South. The split seemed to go from bad to worse during the next two decades: coups, counter-coups, revolutions and counter-revolutions followed one another in succession, as did the old practice of US military intervention, both covert and overt. Much of the hemisphere meanwhile remained comparably poor, despite the work of the Alliance for Progress and similar programs. The economic stagnation in Europe and the United States during the 1970s was followed in Latin America by the so-called lost decade of the 1980s, when the binge of several governments there on petrodollars boomeranged into a prolonged debt crisis.

The end of the lost decade coincided with the end of the Cold War when it appeared that normality had returned to—or at long last could reach—the Americas. The civil wars in Nicaragua and El Salvador had come to an end; Fidel Castro had curbed his adventurism, having now to cope with the loss of his Soviet patron; and the United States, once the jealous hegemon, came to see new promise in what at the time was called "open regionalism" or a "nonexclusive form of territoriality."[86] The Americas would again be seen as a kind of test case. The Canadian, Mexican and US governments enacted the North American Free Trade Agreement (NAFTA) as the beginning of what was imagined to be a hemisphere-wide free trade zone whose efficiencies would boost, rather than compete with, globalization. The OAS and regional diplomacy were energized by former Costa Rican president Oscar Arias and former Colombian president César Gaviria while the inter-American consultative system was rejuvenated by the 1994 Summit of the Americas in Miami, which resulted in some 23 new agreements on subjects from anticorruption to energy to finance. The liberal *Zeitgeist* that went by the name of the Washington Consensus captivated many people in the region as governments raced to privatize state industries, liberalize economies, urbanize hinterlands and gentrify cities.

The results were impressive, but evidently temporary, partial and unpopular in some places. By the following decade a new reaction had set in: Venezuela, Argentina, Bolivia, Ecuador, Nicaragua and Honduras all saw leftist politicians come to power who renounced the Washington Consensus. Brazil, which became one of the world's leading economies in these years, did the same, although with greater success. Latin Americans were taking seriously the calls for "alternative" agreements—e.g., Mercosur, the South American Union (UNASUL), the Andean Community, and the Bolivarian Alliance (ALBA)—touted as rivals to a potential Free Trade Area of the Americas (NAFTA's proposed extension). And by the end of the first decade of the 21st century, bilateral investments and trade flows from Asia had come to make the multiplicity of such projects—open or otherwise—seem, perhaps paradoxically, of even greater importance. "Monogamy is good in marriage," Colombia's finance minister has said, "but not in trade."[87]

Is that true? The question goes to the core of what today constitutes a viable regionalism. Common and complementary interests are not the same, but regions do exist, as do regional patterns in economic, political and even cultural life.[88] The center of gravity today in these areas may indeed be drawing closer to Asia, and so shall Asia be drawn ever closer into American affairs, but this is happening piece by piece, not as a continuous wave. There is little indication so far that a Blaine-style movement is needed to protect the Americas, or to unite them economically so as to better compete with non-American nations and regions, least of all with the rising powers of Asia, whose capital is largely welcomed. This is the paradox of contemporary regionalism: it appears to be so logical in some ways yet can make little sense and be difficult to enact in others.

Americanism perseveres as a project of limited liability and viability. It is more than a pro forma arrangement but it is hardly the force drawing certain societies closer together that some of its promoters have imagined it to be. Europe in this respect is an anomaly, at least for the time being. But even the European Union is neither fully united nor corresponds perfectly to the territory of Europe. What about other "united" regions? The United States is not a region but a nation, as is the United Kingdom, to a lesser extent. If myths have any real-world value, America, the invented world of the past and the future, ought to see great regional potential. Yet in the reality of the present there is no special reason why a set of relatively scattered territories, settled by different empires, treating their indigenous inhabitants quite differently, and being unevenly "developed" should have presented the world's best hope for regional unity. Something more might have been made of the project two-thirds of a century ago, perhaps, but once Europe and parts of Asia set themselves on a course of self-destruction there was little the rest of the world could do but shift its focus there. Nationalism meanwhile has proved too durable and parochial.

Returning to Lord Acton's instrumentalism, one may visualize communities—whether national, regional or global—fostered in order to compensate for more local, social shortcomings, a real product, in other words, of collective volition directed both inward and outward. The appealing thing about regionalism is that it invokes the spirit of nationalism while standing for a supranational—or, in the case of Europe, an antinational—ideal. It has the potential to serve, at least in principle, as Americanism suggests, as a compromise. The danger comes from its potential for violent reversal, as in the former Yugoslavia.

Globalization, however, had clouded the picture, and, along with it, Americanism. The two have become almost equivalent—not in the specific sense of the entire world becoming more like America (or the United States, as it is often alleged with "Americanization" when spoken of synonymously with globalization), but rather with respect to the self-conscious amalgamation of cultures that the Americas have hosted and represented over the course of the past few centuries and that constitutes Americanism's principal contribution to modernity. Does this vitiate a genuinely "American" regionalism? If so it would be a happy irony.

The reason why some communities work and others do not, or why some visions and projects vitiate others—as some have argued recently about the greater West—is almost never clear-cut.[89] Nations and continents never, except in the imagination of some social scientists and military planners, exist with evolutionary predictability. The West's combination of norms, institutions, and political orders had much to do with experimentation in the Americas, which was transmitted back and forth across the Atlantic, less as Canning once described it than as a transnational exchange, amounting, by the end of the 20th century, to a de facto regional history. Yet this Euro-Atlantic area, through its identification with Western civilization, its military preeminence, its mastery, indeed dictation, of the ways of international relations, its hosting and fostering of a transnational elite network and society that became increasingly popular as well, and its leading role in globalization, have all come to function as a kind of archipelago that extends well beyond the Western Hemisphere. It is not yet and probably never will become universal. Its exclaves exist throughout the world as do the enclaves of non-Western communities within the West, almost as though Waldo Frank's island hemisphere were scattered by grapeshot around the world, only to ricochet back again throughout the Americas in hybrid technicolor. Its northern half continues to predominate over the rest. But that is also changing. Today's pan-Americanism is fueled as much by the dramatic growth of the Brazilian and Mexican economies, and by investments by China and other Asian nations throughout the Americas as it is by a residual determination to stand up to Europe, or to the United States, for that matter.

Novelty and change are endemic to America. There is no perfect answer to Crèvecœur's question, and probably never will be. But cultural definitions are subjective and conditional. A better way to understand the American mind and spirit is as an empty (or continually emptying) vessel to be filled in however one likes; in other words, instrumentalist rather than essentialist, stochastic rather than static and structural. The difficulty for Americanism is that multiple vessels are filled differently, at different rates and with different ingredients. Can a mere capacity for novelty or reinvention constitute a regional identity? In other words, is the notion of "America" as being everything Americans want it to be sufficient to bring about a regional culture?

Also, probably not. What then do Americans have in common, really? Taken together, are they merely the various motifs adorning the exterior of the OAS headquarters? There they stand, displayed side by side, impressively, some would say, but hardly constituting a perfect whole. The same might be said about most regions—and regionalisms—at the start of the 21st century.

# Notes

1. E.J. Applewhite, *Washington Itself* (New York: Alfred A. Knopf, 1981), 108-11. For the origins of the OAS' predecessor organization, see Clifford B. Casey, "The Creation and Development of the Pan American Union," *Hispanic American Historical Review* 13, no. 4 (November 1933): 437–56.

2. Alan K. Henrikson, "'A Small, Cozy Town, Global in Scope': Washington, D.C.," *Ekistics: The Problems and Science of Human Settlements* 50, no. 299 (March/April 1983): 123–49.

3. See, *inter alia*, M. J. Bowden, "The Invention of American Tradition," *Journal of Historical Geography* 18, no. 1 (January 1992): 3–26. The effort began with Herbert Bolton's 1932 address to the American Historical Association ("The Epic of Greater America") calling for a single American historiography. For a critique of continentalism, see Eugene Staley, "The Myth of the Continents," *Foreign Affairs* 19, no. 3 (April 1941): 481–93. See also, Arthur P. Whitaker, *The Western Hemisphere Idea: Its Rise and Decline* (Ithaca: Cornell University Press, 1969 ed.), 161–67.

4. J.H. Elliott, *The Old World and the New, 1492–1650* (Cambridge: Cambridge University Press, 2000 [1970]), 3.

5. Martin W. Lewis and Kären E. Wigen, *The Myth of Continents: A Critique of Metageography* (Berkeley: University of California Press, 1997), 1.

6. Whitaker, *Western Hemisphere Idea*, 1, 4. "Common personality" is quoted from an address by John Foster Dulles.

7. Whitaker (*Western Hemisphere Idea*, 7) has claimed that the latter has generally been easier to stomach than the former.

8. See Charles E. Martin, "Regionalism as Illustrated by the Western Hemisphere Solidarity of the Americas," *Social Forces* 21, no. 3 (March 1943): 272–75.

9. Cf. Andrea Oelsner and Antoine Vion, "Friends in the Region: A Comparative Study on Friendship Building in Regional Integration," *International Politics* 48, no. 1 (2011): 129–51.

10. E.g., Viviana Zelizer, "Circuits within Capitalism," in *The Economic Sociology of Capitalism*, ed. Victor Nee and Richard Swedberg (Princeton: Princeton University Press, 2005), 289–322.

11. Cf. Neil Smith, *American Empire: Roosevelt's Geographer and the Prelude to Globalization* (Berkeley: University of California Press, 2004); Kenneth Weisbrode, "The Master, the Maverick and the Machine: Three Wartime Promoters of Peace," *Journal of Policy History* 21, no. 4 (Fall 2009): 366–91.

12. John Keiger, "Raymond Poincaré," in *Mental Maps in the Era of the Two World Wars*, ed. Steven Casey and Jonathan Wright (Basingstoke: Palgrave Macmillan, 2009), 7. Cf. Amitai Etzioni, *Political Unification: A Comparative Study of Leaders and Forces* (New York: Robert E. Krieger Publishing Company, 1974), 6ff.

13. John Lloyd Mecham regarded it as the "world's best example of a regional security arrangement." [*The United States and Inter–American Security, 1889–1960* (Austin: University of Texas Press, 1961), 474.]

14. Joel Garreau, *The Nine Nations of North America* (Boston: Houghton Mifflin, 1981).

15. Daniel J. Boorstin, *America and the Image of Europe: Reflections on American Thought* (Cleveland: The World Publishing Company, 1966), 19, 22.

16. Quoted in L. S. Rowe, et al, "The Pan–American Conferences and Their Significance," *Annals of the American Academy of Political and Social Science* 27, Supplement 17 (May 1906): 14–15.

17. See Eviatar Zerubavel, *Terra Cognita: The Mental Discovery of America* (New Brunswick, N.J.: Rutgers University Press, 1992) and Laura Dassow Walls, *The Passage to Cosmos: Alexander von Humboldt and the Shaping of America* (Chicago: University of Chicago Press, 2009); On the reaction to the Abbé Raynal's *Histoire des deux Indes* (1770), the reputed Bible of the New World: Whitaker, *Western Hemisphere Idea*, 19–20.

18. Whitaker, *Western Hemisphere Idea*, 21.

19. Quoted in Eve Kornfeld, *Creating an American Culture, 1775–1800* (Boston and New York: Bedford/St. Martin's Press, 2001), 20. His emphasis.

20. See, for example, David Armitage and Sanjay Subrahmanyam, eds., *The Age of Revolutions in Global Context. c. 1760–1840* (New York: Palgrave/Macmillan, 2010); C.A. Bayly, *The Birth of the Modern World, 1780–1914: Global Connections and Comparisons* (Malden, MA: Blackwell, 2004); and Doris Garraway, ed., *Tree of Liberty: Cultural Legacies of the Haitian Revolution in the Atlantic World* (Charlottesville: University of Virginia Press, 2008).

21. Tulio Halperín Donghi, *Tradición Española e ideología revolucionaria de Mayo.* (Buenos Aires: Centro Editor de América Latina, 1985), 16ff; Richard Morse, *El espejo de Próspero. Un estudio de la dialéctica del Nuevo Mundo.* (Mexico: Siglo XXI, 1982), 74ff.

22. Arthur P. Whitaker, *The United States and the Independence of Latin America, 1800–1830* (New York: W.W. Norton and Co., 1964), 37.

23. Lester D. Langley, *The Americas in the Age of Revolution, 1750–1850* (New Haven: Yale University Press, 1996).

24. Langley, *Americas in the Age of Revolution,* 3.

25. Langley, *Americas in the Age of Revolution,* 261ff. The first usage of the term "amalgamated" probably dates to the mid-17th century in an Icelandic bishop's reference to the colonists of Greenland: "ad Americae populos se converterunt." [Carl Sauer, *Northern Mists* (San Francisco: Turtle Island Foundation, 1973), 152.]

26. Simon Collier, "Nationality, Nationalism and Supranationalism in the Writings of Simón Bolívar" *Hispanic American Historical Review* 63, no. 1 (February 1983): 40.

27. Cf. Ricaurte Soler, *Idea y cuestión nacional latinoamericanas de la independencia a la emergencia del imperialismo* (Mexico: Siglo Venituno, 1986), 46ff.

28. E.g., Enrique Florescano, ed., *Orígenes y desarrollo de la burguesía en América Latina, 1700–1955* (Mexico: Editorial Nueva Imagen, 1985); Tulio Halperín Donghi, *Revolución y guerra: formación de una élite dirigente en la argentina criolla* (Mexico: Siglo Ventiuno, 1979); Joyce Appleby, *Capitalism and a New Social Order: The Republican Vision of the 1790s* (New York: New York University Press, 1984).

29. Francisco Valdés–Ugalde, "Janus and the Northern Colossus: Perceptions of the United States in the Building of the Mexican Nation," *Journal of American History* 86, no. 2 (September 1999): 575.

30. Cf. Morse, *El espejo de Próspero,* 9–10, 22–29, 169ff.

31. Hugo Torrano, *Rodó: acción y libertad* (Montevideo: Barreiro y Ramos, S.A., 1973), 237–38; cf. Carlos Real de Azúa's prologue in: José Enrique Rodó, *Ariel y Motivos de Proteo* (Cuarta Transversal de Boleíta, Venezuela: Biblioteca Ayacucho, 1976), xxii–xxxi.

32. Roberto Fernández Retamar makes this point about Rodó and even more pointedly about Martí in a 1971 essay: "Caliban: Notes Toward a Discussion of Culture in Our America" in *Caliban and Other Essays*, trans. Lynn Garafola, David Arthur McMurray, and Roberto Márquez (Minneapolis: University of Minnesota Press, 1989), 21–23.

33. Jean Franco, *The Modern Culture of Latin America: Society and the Artist* (New York: Frederick A. Praeger Publishers, 1967), 13–14; cf. Leopoldo Zea: "The Latin American mind . . . is an entirely modern one." [Harry Bernstein, review of *The Latin American Mind*, by Leopoldo Zea, *Hispanic American Historical Review* 44, no. 3 (August 1964): 397]; Zea, *América Latina y el mundo* (Buenos Aires: Eudeba, 1965), 20ff.

34. Rubén Darío, *Selected Poems of Rubén Darío*, trans. Lysander Kemp (Austin: University of Texas Press, 1965), 69–70.

35. José Martí, "Mother America," *El Partido Liberal* (Mexico, April 12, 1889), trans. Elinor Randall, in *Our America: Writings on Latin America and the Struggle for Cuban Independence by José Martí*, Philip S. Foner, ed. (New York: Monthly Review Press, 1977), 74–79. The article was a speech given by Martí on the occasion of the 1889 pan-American Congress.

36. Enrique Krauze, *Redeemers: Ideas and Power in Latin America*, trans. Hank Heifetz (New York: HarperCollins, 2011), 9, 33.

37. Emilio Gentile, "Impending Modernity: Fascism and the Ambivalent Image of the United States," *Journal of Contemporary History* 28, no. 1 (January 1993): 7.

38. See Richard V. Salisbury, "Hispanismo versus Pan Americanism: Spanish Efforts to Counter U.S. Influence in Latin America before 1930," in David Sheinin, ed., *Beyond the Ideal: Pan Americanism in Inter-American Affairs* (Westport: Praeger, 2000), 67–77. For the transition from longitude to latitude, see Jay Sexton, *The Monroe Doctrine* (New York: Hill and Wang, 2011), 8–13.

39. Morse, *El espejo de Próspero*, 8ff; Lewis and Wigen, *Myth of Continents*, 181–82. Cf. Sexton, *Monroe Doctrine*, 136–37 (predating the reference). For another precedent in the thought of the Abbé de Pradt, see Whitaker, *United States and the Independence of Latin America*, 102–5.

40. This is the main argument of Morse (*El espejo de Próspero*, 154–69), who reflects Rodó's mirror back upon itself. See also José David Saldívar, *The Dialectics of America: Geneology, Cultural Critique, and Literary History* (Durham: Duke University Press, 1991). The most recent, widely read attempt to polemicize these questions is Walter D. Mignolo's *The Idea of Latin America* (Oxford: Blackwell, 2005).

41. Emily S. Rosenberg, "World War I and 'Continental Solidarity,'" *The Americas* 31, no. 3 (January 1975): 313–34 ; See also Joseph Tulchin, *The Aftermath of War: World War I and U.S. Policy Toward Latin America* (New York: New York University Press, 1971); Julius Klein, "The Monroe Doctrine as a Regional Understanding," *Hispanic American Historical Review* 4, no. 2 (May 1921): 248–55; Whitaker, *Western Hemisphere Idea*, 112–14.

42. Wolfgang Schivelbusch, *Three New Deals: Reflections on Roosevelt's America, Mussolini's Italy, and Hitler's Germany* (New York: Picador, 2007), 4–11.

43. Louis L. Snyder, *Macro-Nationalisms: A History of the Pan Movements* (Westport, CT: Greenwood Press, 1984).

44. Cf. Prasenjit Duara, "The Discourse of Civilization and Pan–Asianism," *Journal of World History* 12, no. 1 (2001): 99–130.

45. E.g., Jacinta O'Hagan, *Conceptualizing the West in International Relations: From Spengler to Said* (Basingstoke: Palgrave Macmillan, 2002), 60–65, 83–89, 105–6. Similarly inspired theories focusing on the Americas include Walter Prescott Webb's "great frontier" and the seven major "culture worlds" of the geographers Richard Russell and Fred Kniffen, and F. S. C. Northrop's *The Taming of the Nations*. See Jorge Basadre, review of Whitaker's *Western Hemisphere Idea*, *Hispanic American Historical Review* 35, no. 2 (May 1955): 285.

46. See esp. vol. 4, *The American Spirit* (Macmillan, 1942), 10–61: "Civilization—Center of Interest." The reference to Spengler is on page 65; to Freud on page 510.

47. Charles Beard, "Americans in Mexico," *New Republic* 48, October 13, 1926, 225–26.

48. Dardo Cuneo, *Aventura y letra de América Latina* (Caracas: Monte Ávila Editores, 1975), 213; *The Memoirs of Waldo Frank*, ed. Alan Trachtenberg (Amherst: University of Massachusetts Press, 1973).

49. Waldo Frank, *South American Journey* (New York: Duell, Sloan and Pearce, 1943), 369–70. The exposition of the "island hemisphere" also appeared in the April 1943 issue of *Foreign Affairs*. One year earlier, he published his *Virgin Spain*, which he dedicated to "those brother Americans/whose tongues are Spanish and Portuguese/whose homes are between the Rio Grande/and Tierra del Fuego/but whose America/like mine/stretches from the Arctic to the Horn." The point about legitimacy comes from Laurie Kay Sommers, "The Creation of 'Hispanic' Panethnicity in the United States," *Journal of American Folklore* 104, no. 411 (Winter 1991): 34.

50. *The Memoirs of Waldo Frank*, 123.

51. David Armitage, "Three Concepts of Atlantic History," in *The British in the Atlantic World 1500–1800*, ed. David Armitage and Michael J. Braddick (Houndmills: Palgrave Macmillan, 2002), and Bernard Bailyn, *Atlantic History: Concepts and Contours* (Cambridge, MA: Harvard University Press, 2005). For a different perspective, see Nicolás Wey Gómez, *The Tropics of Empire: Why Columbus Sailed South to the Indies* (Cambridge, MA: MIT Press, 2008).

52. For this and the idea of multiple Wests, see Peter J. Katzenstein, "The West as Anglo-America: Plural and Pluralist," (presentation at the 2010 Annual Meeting of the American Political Science Association, Washington D.C., September 2–5, 2010).

53. Clarence K. Streit, "The Atlantic Union Plan and the Americas," *Annals of the American Academy of Political and Social Science* 204 (July 1939): 94.

54. Clarence K. Streit, *Union Now! A Proposal for a Federal Union of the Democracies of the North Atlantic* (New York: Harper & Brothers Publishers, 1939), 197.

55. Walter Lippmann, *U.S. Foreign Policy: Shield of the Republic* (Boston: Little, Brown and Company, 1943), 122–23.

56. Walter Lippmann, "Second Thoughts on Havana," *Foreign Affairs* 6, no. 4 (July 1928): 545; cf. Carleton Beals, *Pan America: A Program for the Western Hemisphere* (Boston: Houghton Mifflin Co., 1940); Duncan Aikman, *The All-American Front* (New York: Doubleday, 1940).

57. Quoted in Alfred Coester, "Practical Pan Americanism," *Hispania* 10, no. 2 (March 1927): 95–98. In international law in the Americas, the term comes from the Lansing-Ishii Treaty of 1917.

58. *Selected Writings of Bolivar*, vol. 1, trans. Lewis Bertrand (New York: The Colonial Press Inc., 1951), 118. See also Josef L. Kunz, "The Idea of 'Collective Security' in Pan-American Developments," *Western Political Quarterly* 6, no. 4 (December 1953): 660–61; Whitaker, *Western Hemisphere Idea*, 25–27.

59. See J. Fred Rippy, "Pan–Hispanic Propaganda in Hispanic America," *Political Science Quarterly* 37, no. 3 (September 1922): 402ff. Joseph B. Lockey ("An Early Pan-American Scheme," *Pacific Historical Review* 2, no. 4: 439–47), discusses the 1812 suggestion of William Shaler for five confederations: 1. California and Mexico; 2. New Granada, Venezuela and Quito; 3. Peru; 4. Argentina, Uruguay, Paraguay, Bolivia, and Chile; and 5. Brazil.

60. Whitaker, *United States and the Independence of Latin America*, 95–100.

61. Whitaker, *United States and the Independence of Latin America*, 43; and Whitaker, *Western Hemisphere Idea*, 27–31.

62. William R. Castle, "The Monroe Doctrine and Pan-Americanism," *Annals of the American Academy of Political and Social Science* 204 (July 1939): 111.

63. Ernest May, *The Making of the Monroe Doctrine* (Cambridge, MA: Harvard University Press, 1975).

64. Sexton, *Monroe Doctrine*, chps. 5, 6.

65. Whitaker, *United States and the Independence of Latin America*, 518.

66. Paraphrase of Ezequiel Padilla (on rivers) in Graham H. Stuart, review of *Free Men of America* by Ezequiel Padilla in *Hispanic American Historical Review* 24, no. 1 (February 1944): 135. cf. Charles Lyon Chandler, "The Pan American Origin of the Monroe Doctrine," *American Journal of International Law* 8, no. 3 (July 1914): 515–19.

67. Whitaker, *Western Hemisphere Idea*, 41.

68. For summaries of these and subsequent gatherings, see Samuel Guy Inman, *Inter-American Conferences, 1826–1954: History and Problems* (Washington, D.C.: The University Press of Washington and the Community College Press, 1965) and Charles G. Fenwick, *The Inter-American Regional System*, Holy Cross College, Fenwick Lectures (New York: McMullen, 1949).

69. Javier Corrales and Richard E. Feinberg, "Regimes of Cooperation in the Western Hemisphere: Power Interests and Intellectual Traditions," *International Studies Quarterly* 43, no. 1 (March 1999): 5.

70. John Anthony Caruso, "The Pan American Railway," *Hispanic American Historical Review* 31, no. 4 (November 1951): 608–39.

71. Russell H. Bastert, "A New Approach to the Origins of Blaine's Pan American Policy," *Hispanic American Historical Review* 39, no. 3 (August 1959): 375.

72. Josef L. Kunz, review of *El pensamiento internacional de Alberdi* by Isidoro Ruiz Moreno, Jr, *American Journal of International Law* 40, no. 2 (April 1946): 501–3; A. Curtis Wilgus, "James G. Blaine and the Pan American Movement," *Hispanic American Historical Review* 5, no. 4 (November 1922): 662–708; Mark T. Gilderhus, "Forming an Informal Empire without Colonies: U.S.-Latin American Relations," *Latin American Research Review* 40, no. 3 (October 2005): 312–25; Soler, *Idea y cuestión nacional latinoamericanas,* 182–86.

73. See Alonso Aguilar, *Pan Americanism from Monroe to the Present: A View from the Other Side,* trans. Asa Zatz (New York: Monthly Review Press, 1968); J.B. Atkins, "European Views of Pan-America," *North American Review* (June 1928): 687–92.

74. Quoted in Whitaker, *Western Hemisphere Idea,* 84.

75. Nabuco was one of the most pro-US of South Americans and a close friend of the statesman and lawyer Elihu Root. On the subject of art in the United States, he noted, "while the English is solid and the French graceful, yours is clean–cut. There is an American perfection, as characteristic as the Japanese, which I believe is well defined by the word 'clean-cut.'" [Nabuco, "The Share of America in Civilization," *Hispanic American Historical Review* 15, no. 1 (October 1909): 62.]

76. Quoted by Mark T. Gilderhus, *Pan American Visions: Woodrow Wilson in the Western Hemisphere 1913–1921* (Tucson: University of Arizona Press, 1986), 60.

77. Paraphrase of Blaine in: Joseph B. Lockey, "The Meaning of Pan-Americanism," *American Journal of International Law* 19, no. 1 (January 1925): 109.

78. Carlos Dávila, *We of the Americas* (Chicago and New York: Ziff–Davis, 1949), 171.

79. Carlton J. H. Hayes, "The American Frontier—Frontier of What?" *American Historical Review* 51, no. 2 (January 1946): 203–4, 212.

80. Quoted in Gilderhus, *Pan American Visions,* 3.

81. Gilderhus, *Pan American Visions,* ix.

82. Quoted in Krauze, *Redeemers*, 40.

83. Quoted in Gilderhus, *Pan American Visions*, 54.

84. Lippmann, "Second Thoughts on Havana," 543. Lippmann had accompanied Morrow on his Mexican mission.

85. Bryce Wood, *The Making of the Good Neighbor Policy* (New York: Columbia University Press, 1961), 4ff; cf. Mark T. Gilderhus review of *Good Neighbor Diplomacy: United States Policies on Latin America 1933–1945* by Irwin F. Gellman, *The Americas* 37, no. 4 (April 1981): 551–53.

86. John Gerard Ruggie, "Territoriality and Beyond: Problematizing Modernity in International Relations," *International Organization* 47, no. 1 (1992): 139–74.

87. "The Pacific Players Go to Market," *The Economist*, April 9, 2011; Andrés Oppenheimer, "2012 Will Be Anything But Boring in the Americas," *Miami Herald*, December 24, 2011. For description of the various groupings, see Efe Can Gürcan, "New Regionalisms and Radical Identity Formation in Latin America: Towards an 'Alter-Global' Paradigm." *Journal of Social Research & Policy* 1, no. 2 (December 2010): 19–33.

88. Cf. Jorge Castañeda, "Pan-Americanism and Regionalism: A Mexican View" *International Organization* 10, no. 3 (August 1956): 373–89.

89. See, *inter alia*, the structuralist account by Ulrich Krotz, "The (Beginning of the) End of the Political Unity of the West? Four Scenarios of North Atlantic Futures" EUI Working Papers RSCAS 2008/31 (Robert Schuman Centre for Advanced Studies, European University Institute, 2008).